The West Country is a Garden

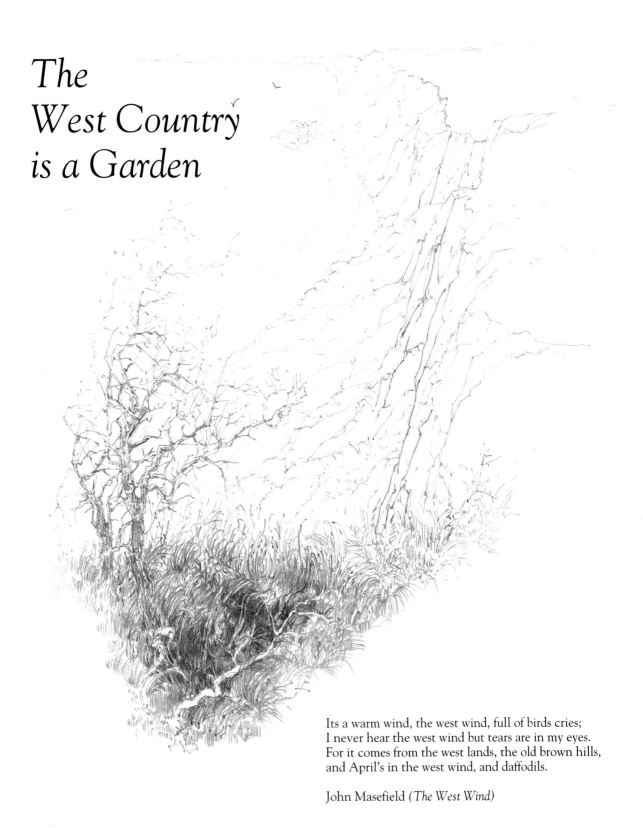

Its a warm wind, the west wind, full of birds cries;
I never hear the west wind but tears are in my eyes.
For it comes from the west lands, the old brown hills,
and April's in the west wind, and daffodils.

John Masefield (*The West Wind*)

Bickleigh, Devon

FLOWERING CHERRY *(Prunus kwansan)*

The West Country is a Garden

A wayfarer's companion

Catherine Hamilton

Dedication

For Morwenna Chynoweth

Acknowledgements

I am deeply grateful to many people who, by their kindness, friendship, and willingness to share their great love of flowers and historical heritage, made the work for this book not only possible but an event of great joy.

My special thanks to Anne Barnes, Gladys and Michael Beattie, Roger and Nick Burley, K.F. Brown, H. Catling, George Kirkby, Lord and Lady Tranmire, Mary and the late Tom Cook, Alan Newton, Dr and Mrs Delap, Miss E. Webb, Jacquie Spiers, Frances Lonsbrough, Margaret Baynton, Jean Spiceley, Janette and Bill Chynoweth and family, and the Garden Staff of Morrab Gardens, Cornwall.

A very special thank you to my sister and travelling companion, Bernadette Spiers for her patient, enthusiastic assistance, to the late Ruth and Bob Hamilton, and Eileen and Lew Fell who looked after my children whilst I was away on my journey; and finally, David Bateman, for continued confidence in my ability.

This edition published in 2004 by
Greenwich Editions
The Chrysalis Building
Bramley Road, London W10 6SP

An imprint of **Chrysalis** Books Group plc

ISBN 0 86288 544 2

Printed and bound in China

Design by David Bateman Ltd

Contents

Introduction

For any artist, a journey through the West Country of England is magical. The diverse landscape, architecture, climatic atmosphere, all in an ancient setting, provide enough material for any artistic work. For me, principally a flower painter, the opportunity to portray the flora of the area, both wild and cultivated, was a delightful bonus.

Enjoying the freedom of my publisher's brief— "Rent a campervan and wander around England — paint and sketch anything that catches your eye", here in the West Country I found my way (often by sheer navigational mishap) to many areas rarely if ever visited by tourists. On many occasions, I was able to share my love of nature, flowers and gardens with the locals, overcoming any barriers of reserve.

The strength, beauty, colour and seemingly endless variety of flowers, plants and trees throughout the West Country is just amazing. Whether growing near or by majestic Cathedrals, castles or tiny thatched cottages, prehistoric stone relics, lonely moors, rugged cliffs, sandy bays or bygone smugglers' coves, they all seemed to weave together, creating a rich and vibrant tapestry of natural splendour.

I hope that my choice and portrayal of sketches and paintings will enable the reader, whether a local or a visitor, to share some of my wonderful experiences in this unique part of England — the West Country.

Salisbury Cathedral, Wiltshire

HYPERICUM (Rose of Sharon — St John's wort) (*Hypericum calycinum*)
HOLLYHOCK (*Alcea*)
DELPHINIUM (*Delphinium hybr.*)

What better place to begin an exploration of the West Country than from New Sarum, the original name of Salisbury? As I approached, it seemed the Cathedral spire soared directly from the meadows. Indeed, it is the highest in England at 404 feet; the Cathedral, the only one built to a single plan, is a marvel of design and engineering, even today, yet it was built between 1220 and 1258 and the spire completed in 1380.

The flowers I painted were all growing in or near the ancient Cathedral Close, the largest and finest in the country with its fascinating variety of architecture blending with the graceful cathedral to form one of the most beautiful cities in the world.

Nearby is Britain's most famous ancient
monument — Stonehenge. It took a
thousand years to build and was
completed about 3200 years ago, almost a
thousand years after the Avebury rings.
By then its builders probably had
primitive mechanical assistance which they would have needed, for not only were the uprights
and lintels slotted together, but the earliest blue stones were probably dragged 200 miles from
Wales. Most of the stones we see today came from the Marlborough Downs.

My painting of wild English daisies is significant because it is thought Stonehenge was the
sanctuary of a sun-worshipping cult. The origin of daisy is "Deus Eyes" — "the Eyes of God"
through which He watched over man, a belief from ancient sun-worship probably derived from
the daisy's habit of opening its petals to the first rays of the sun and closing them at sunset.

Stonehenge, Wiltshire

WILD ENGLISH DAISY (*Bellis perennis*)

These are four of the stones, which together with the ditches between them, make the largest layout of prehistoric ritual stones in Europe — the Avebury rings. Constructed some 4000 years ago, the task of digging the ditches and moving the stones three miles from the Marlborough Downs without machines or even the wheel, is mind boggling! The stones, weighed up to 60 tonnes! I learned that they were not carved in any way but must have been chosen for their natural shape and size. I could not resist sketching some of them, nor painting the sofr toadstools growing close by — such a contrast in shape and life-span.

Avebury, Wiltshire

TOADSTOOLS *(Fly agaric)*

Near Colne in north Wiltshire, I sketched the Cherhill Horse, cut in the chalk downs in 1780 by a Dr Alsop who is said to have directed his workmen from a mile or so away by shouting through a megaphone. His white horse is 140 feet long.

There can be few lovelier sights .than a field of poppies.

The Cherhill Horse, near Colne, Wiltshire

FIELD POPPY *(Papaver rhoeas)*

Brokerswood is my kind of place. A variety of walks meander through 120 acres of rich woodland park. As well as over fifty different trees, there is a myriad of bird life, including herons and kingfishers at the lake.

I chose to paint two trees in flower — the ash and the monkshood, both so delicate.

Brokerswood Woodland Park, Wiltshire

ASH *(Fraxinus excelsior)*
MONKSHOOD *(Aconitum napellus)*

I must confess I had never heard of
a "bird garden" until I came across
the Tropical Bird Gardens at Rode.
There I found over 200
species, from cranes to minute
finches, and, unbelievably, a flock
of macaws. They fly free in this
beautiful setting; the picturesque
flamingos and irises in particular
caught my eye.

Tropical Bird Gardens, Rode, Wiltshire

YELLOW FLAG (*Iris pseudacorus*)
GREATER FLAMINGO
   (*Phoenicopterus ruber*)

There is only one word for
Stourhead Gardens — magnificent
— surely one of the finest in
Europe. I walked for a mile and a
half from the stately house, down
to the lake edged with many
varieties of rhododendrons and
azaleas, across the stone bridge,
through the grotto and past the
Pantheon up to the woodland
sheltered stone rotunda of the
Temple of the Sun. A spectacular
tour of gardens, laid out in 1742.
I wanted to record it all — but
settled for the Pantheon and
rhododendrons.

The Pantheon
Stourhead Gardens, Wiltshire

RHODODENDRON

My first stop in Thomas Hardy's beloved Dorset was at Tolpuddle. There I sketched the sycamore tree, under which six farmers met in 1834 and formed a society to fight against their "starvation" wages. For this they were transported to Australia. However, they were reprieved eventually and became known as the Tolpuddle Martyrs. In 1934 The Trades Union Congress built a row of cottages in the village as a memorial and each July there is a service and parade. The roadside shelter also shown in my sketch was built from the timbers of H.M.S. Hercules.

Tolpuddle Village, Dorset

SYCAMORE (*Acer pseudoplatanus*)

16

Badbury Rings was originally an Iron Age fort, and later became a Roman stronghold. When the Romans withdrew a town developed but the area within the rings, which can be seen distinctly from the air, has been deserted for a thousand years except for picnickers and sightseers who climb to the summit to admire the view of three counties and the sea.

Bradbury Rings, Dorset

DORSET HEATH *(Erica ciliaris)*

This must be one of the most beautiful and extensive private gardens, owned, lived in and tended by one family, that is open to the public. Although only developed from open heathland in 1914, it is now as mature as many begun a century or more before.

It comprises a unique series of separate gardens, designed so that only one can be seen at a time. I browsed through the restful dignity and peace of Italian, Roman, Japanese, English, rock, water, woodland and sub-tropical gardens, as well as enjoying the elevated views of Poole harbour and the many birds.

Torre Gate in the Japanese Garden at Compton Acres, Poole, Dorset
MAGNOLIA (Magnolia soulangiana)
MEXICAN ORANGE BLOSSOM (Choisya ternata)
ROBIN (Erithacus rubecula)

Not far from Compton Acres is Lulworth Cove, almost enclosed by hills and consequently almost lake-like in its serenity. Walks in both directions along the cliff top give spectacular views including Durdle Door, a limestone arch which I have drawn, and lead to a fascinating forest of fossilised trees. The small butterfly, Lulworth skipper, is unique to the cliffs above the cove where it was first recorded a century ago.

And do not leave the area without sampling a tea with "Dorset Nobs", so called after the buttons they resemble; making the buttons has long been a local cottage industry.

Lulworth Cove, Dorset

LULWORTH SKIPPER (*Thymelicus acteon*)
ROCK SAMPHIRE (*Crithmum maritimum*)
FOSSILISED TREE TRUNK

Iwerne Minster, including its village pump, was restored by its rich owner early this century. Today, many of the buildings are individually owned, still well preserved, and "cottage" flowers abound. The Norman church has a 15th-century spire, unusual in Dorset, and there is a Roman villa site just outside the village.

Village pump, Iwerne Minster, Dorset

STOCK (*Matthiola incana*)

One of the West Country's best beauty spots is Lyme Regis. It was given the royal suffix in the 13th century by Edward I who used its harbour when fighting the French. The town and harbour are ringed by multi-coloured cliffs of layered lime and clay, beautiful but notoriously unstable. Jane Austin had a seaside cottage here.

Round cottages are nor uncommon in Dorset. The one I sketched was named after the shape of its thatched roof.

Umbrella Cottage, Lyme Regis, Dorset

FORGET-ME-NOT (*Myosotis arvensis*)
DIANTHUS (*Dianthus plumarius*)

High-banked country lanes lead to Sandford Orchas, a small village in a valley not far from Sherborne. There you will find a complete Tudor manor house guarded by a charming, well preserved gatehouse. When I was there, many flowers softened the brick wall and I spent a happy hour or so sketching and painting.

Gatehouse, Sandford Orchas, Dorset

TAGETES (*Tagetes patula*)
HEARTSEASE (*Viola tricolor*)

23

Butterflies hold a deep fascination for me and I wrote and illustrated a book about those found in my native New Zealand. So a visit to the butterfly farm at Compton House was inevitable. Butterflies and moths from all over the world are bred and reared for collection, study, conservation and release in flower gardens. They can be seen at all stages of growth and when conditions are right, fluttering in the trees surrounding the house.

Compton House, Over Compton, Dorset

SWALLOWTAIL (*Papilio machaon britannicus*)
PURPLE EMPEROR (*Apaturo iris*)
BRITISH LARGE BLUE (*Maculinea arion*)
LANTANA (*Lantana camara*)

In a gap in the Purbeck Hills stand the ruins of Corfe Castle (corfe means gap). It has been a ruin since Oliver Cromwell destroyed it in 1646. Its origins are unknown, but it is certain that 18-year-old King Edward the Martyr was murdered there in 987. Some of the buildings in the village below were constructed of stone from the castle in the 17th and 18th centuries.

Corfe Castle, Dorset

COMMON MALLOW (*Malva sylvestris*)
WILD RHODODENDRON (*Rhododendron ponticum*)

Thomas Hardy's cottage provides for me the perfect
memory of the romantic Dorset countryside. The
great novelist's stories set in the county haunt me
and this simple, rafted, whitewashed cottage make
the ideal memorial.

Thomas Hardy's Cottage, Higher Brockhampton, Dorset

BLUEBELLS (*Endymion nonscriptus*)

Forde Abbey dates from 1138 when the
Cistercian order of monks founded it. It
houses a very fine collection of tapestries
and stands in 15 acres of beautiful
gardens. I painted one of the magnificent
camellias.

Forde Abbey, Somerset

CAMELLIA (*Contessa, Lavinia Maggi*)

Exmoor is an area of contrast and everchanging mood; of gorse,
heather and bilberry covered moorland, and coombs wooded with
birch, mountain ash, alder and scrub oak. There are small villages
with whitewashed cottages and relics of ancient settlements — truly
an artist's delight! The small market town of Dunster is dominated by
a castle owned by only two families over a thousand years. I drew the
17th-century yarn market which stands in the centre of the town.

Exmoor, Somerset and Devon

The Yarn Market, Dunster, Somerset

WESTERN GORSE (*Ulex galii*)
BILBERRY (*Vaccinium myrtilis*)

31

If you like to conjure up images of chivalrous knights, then the extensive earthworks which are all that remains of Cadbury Castle, is the place to do it, for it is considered by some to be the site of Camelot, the seat of King Arthur and his Knights of the Round Table. Certainly excavation has revealed evidence of Neolithic occupation; there are also traces from Roman times and the Dark Ages when Arthur ruled.

Cadbury Castle, South Cadbury, Somerset

Ancient coin minted at Cadbury

BLACKBERRY (*Rubus fruticosus*)

I am intrigued by the unusual, so determined to sketch the
Abbot's Fish House at Mere about which I had read. Mere was
the site of one of the Iron Age lake villages in the area.
Another was nearby Glastonbury, built on marshland beside
navigable water on platforms of brushwood and timber, where
later the famous abbey was built. The 14th-century fish house
was used by the abbot's water bailiff for the supply of fish to
the Glastonbury monks.

It is believed the Romans first planted apple trees in
Britain. Somerset abounds in apple orchards, and cider has
been brewed for centuries. Hence my painting of apple
blossom.

Abbot's Fish House, Meare, Somerset

APPLE BLOSSOM

Wells Cathedral, Somerset

Bishop's Palace, Wells, Somerset

SHASTA DAISY (*Chrysanthemum maximum*)

Small but exquisite — that is Wells Cathedral. Surrounded by trees, shrubs and flowers, partnered by the Bishop's Palace, an early 13th-century fortified house protected by a moat, the Cathedral quarter provides a veritable haven from the hustle and bustle of the city; its light industries include the famous Cheddar cheese factories. Built from the end of the 12th to the middle of the 14th century, the Cathedral's west front contains the finest collection of medieval ecclesiastical sculpture in the country.

For all its remarkable history and the beauty of its buildings, it is the floral displays in Bath that have remained uppermost in my mind.

Like most visitors, my imagination was stimulated by the Roman Baths and I could see the centurions, the merchants and their ladies, using the elaborate system of spring water and steam for their therapeutic benefit. I pictured the crowning of Edgar, the first King of England, towards the end of the 10th century, in the original Abbey built by the Saxons. What a proud setting for the contrasting colours of the fuchsia, petunia, geranium, hydrangea, pansies and the multitude of other flowers displayed in gay hanging baskets, pole gardens, window boxes and tubs.

Pole Garden, Stall Street, Bath, Avon

FUCHSIA "PINK QUARTET"

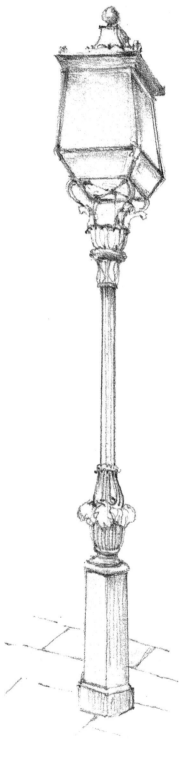

The floral emblem of Bristol since medieval times, the scarlet "Flower of Bristowe", also known as The Maltese Cross or nonsuch, was brought to England by merchants returning from eastern Mediterranean lands when Bristol was Bristowe.

I was fascinated by this street lamp standing outside the Corn Exchange.

Old Street Lamp, Corn Street, Bristol, Avon

THE FLOWER OF BRISTOWE (*Lychnis chalcedonica*)

The long, deep valley of the River Dart provides Dartmouth with a very mild climate in which flowers can bloom as late as December. It also has a deep water harbour which has been used as an assembly point for many war fleets, including those of the 1147 and 1190 Crusades, and the American Navy in 1944. The Royal Naval College overlooks the river and the town with its narrrow streets and ancient buildings. There are two 15th- and one 16th-century castles.

Agincourt House, Dartmouth, Devon

CLEMATIS (*Clematis montana Elizabeth*)

For me, Dartmoor's wild beauty is very special. The variety of
landscape and colour is remarkable — a haze of gentle purples, soft
browns and olives, broken by giant rugged outcrops of granite tors
sculptured by centuries of weathering. And, in the coombs and folds in
the hills, lie the quaint towns and villages, many of which were linked
by clapper bridges built in the 13th century to span streams when the
frequent sudden storms common in the area produced flash floods.

Morning mist over Dartmoor, Devon

Clapper Bridge, Postbridge

HEATHER (*Calluna vulgaris*)

Many of the ancient buildings of Exeter were destroyed by bombs in 1942 but the great Norman Cathedral of St Mary and St Peter survived, despite severe damage. By its 600th anniversary, celebrated in 1969, it had been lovingly repaired and, since then, further restoration has made it one of the most colourful and warmest cathedrals in the kingdom. It was fitting that I should find these rich, velvet textured pansies growing in window boxes in the Close.

The Choir Chancel, Exeter Cathedral, Devon

PANSIES (*Viola witrrockiana*)

44

Garden owners are such a generous breed! By invitation I gathered these flowers during an evening stroll through Honiton, one of the gateways to Devon. I used the ancient town as a base from which to explore neighbouring villages and countryside, and was fascinated by its famous Honiton lace, pottery and buildings like this very old flour mill which, until 30 years ago, had been in constant use for generations.

Old Mill Wheel, Honiton, Devon

CALENDULA (*Calendula officinalis*)
CARNATION (*Dianthus caryophyllus*)
SWEET WILLIAM (*D. barbatus*)
LOVE-IN-A-MIST (*Nigella damascena*)
EVENING PRIMROSE (*Oenothera missouriensis*)

Although found in other parts of the south of England, Devon lanes and hedgerows have a particular character and romance of their own. They are possibly a relic of Norman times, when most of the county was a royal forest, and the deer and other wildlife protected game. The farmers banked and hedged-in their fields with anything to hand to protect their crops from the deer. Today they are unique nature reserves for a rich collection of flora and fauna. My favourite is the Devon primrose — there is no other as lovely.

A high-banked Devon hedgerow and lane

PRIMROSE (*Primula vulgaris*)
WILD STRAWBERRY (*Fragaria vesca*)

The parish church's 14th-century granite tower soars from the centre
of Widecombe-in-the-Moor seeming to search for the Dartmoor sky in
stark contrast to the rolling moorland beyond. It is ironic that the
subjects of the wellknown song about the Widecombe Fair, still held
annually in September, were all from another parish — old Uncle Tom
Cobleigh an' all, and his grey mare!

Widecombe-in-the-Moor

DOG ROSE (*Rosa canina*)
PERIWINKLE (*Vinca minor*)
STITCHWORT (*Stellaria graminea*)
RED CAMPION (*Silene dioica*)
LORDS AND LADIES
or CUCKOO PINT (*Arum maculatum*)

49

The Victorian resort of Lynton sits 500 feet above the old
fishing village of Lynmouth. Together they form one of the
prettiest spots in north Devon. They are linked by a curious
funicular railway, opened in 1890, which uses water ballast to
counterbalance the two cars as they ascend and descend.

Cottages in Lynmouth, Devon

Funicular rail car linking Lynmouth and Lynton

NASTURTIUM (*Tropaeolum minus*)
HONESTY (*Lunaria annua*)

Barnstaple people say their town was granted a charter in 930 and is consequently one of the oldest boroughs in England. It did mint its own coins in the late 10th century and was an important cloth manufacturing and ship building centre until the estuary of the river Taw began to silt up, causing a decline in its standing as a merchant centre.

The town has some good Georgian architecture of which Queen Anne's Walk is an excellent example.

Queen Anne's Walk, Barnstaple, Devon
TULIPS (*Tulipa*)

I had a truly magical walk through the mile-long Lydford Gorge. The twisting paths, carpeted on either side by wild garlic, lichens, moss, and ferns, are almost roofed by magnificent oaks. It was said to be the hideout of the Gubbins Gang, 17th-century highway robbers of considerable ill-repute.

Lydford Gorge, Devon

ENGLISH OAK (*Quercus robur*)

Probably one of the most painted and photographed fishing villages in Britain is Clovelly. It is described as "a village like a waterfall" because its streets tumble so steeply from the cliff top to the little harbour below. No cars are allowed and donkeys deliver goods to the shops. The cottages are gay with window boxes and tiny gardens. An enchanting place.

Clovelly, Devon

WISTERIA (*Wisteria sinensis*)
GERANIUM (*Pelargonium zonal form*)
FUCHSIA (*Fuchsia fulgens hybrid*)

The smallest of the West Country moors, Bodmin is, nevertheless, as full of contrast as either Dartmoor or Exmoor. The remotest parts can only be reached by horse or on foot and are bleak, wind-eroded, wild, upland areas. But there is also a gentle side of rolling hills, green fields, woods and hedgerows, where summer flowers and grasses dust the moor with subtle colours. There are many places of historic interest and beauty.

Bodmin was the only town in Cornwall in 1086 and was on the main trade route from Ireland to Europe. The name means "abode of monks" and the town developed around the priory built by followers of St Perroc, who settled there in the 5th century. St Petroc's Church is the largest in Cornwall and contains a remarkable 12th-century stone font with an elaborately carved bowl, almost three feet in diameter.

Bodmin Moor

12th-century stone font, St Petroc's Church, Bodmin, Cornwall

COMMON COTTON GRASS (*Eriophorum angustifolium*)

WILD CARROT (*Daucus carota*)
BUTTERCUP (*Ranunculus acris*)

In Cornwall's northernmost parish of
Morwenstow, just a few yards from the steep,
rugged cliffs rising from the surging Atlantic
Ocean, is the church of St Morwenna and
St John the Baptist. Among the gravestones
in the daisy and buttercup strewn grass
stands the figurehead from the sailing ship
Caledonia, wrecked on the rocks below in
1842. Her captain is buried immediately
below this unusual monument.

Another possible site of King Arthur's Camelot is Tintagel Castle. The ruined walls of a 12th-century castle cling tenuously to the cliffs of the headland, now almost separated from the mainland. A heady atmosphere this — but who knows? Was it here or Cadbury the king held court? I was charmed by the Old Post Office in Tinragel village, a small 14th-century stone house built as a medieval manor and owned by the National Trust.

The Old Post Office, Tintagel, Cornwall

WILD THYME (*Thymus praecox*)
SPRING SQUILL (*Scilla verna*)

I think I agree with people who say that Mousehole is the least spoiled and most genuine fishing village in Cornwall. I dallied there for some rime and tried to imagine its sacking by Spanish raiders in 1595. What a contrast to the tranquil scene I enjoyed. It has an interesting bird hospital now run by the S.P.C.A.

Mousehole, Cornwall

GANNET (*Sula bassana*)
ROSE (*Rosa gallica*)

Put Godolphin House high on your list of places to see. It has an atmosphere of its own. Parts were built in the 15th century and the Godolphin family lived in it for 200 years. I loved the 16th-century north front with its mullioned windows and granite columns.
I found growing wild nearby an old Burnet rose — its fragrant creamy white flowers providing a nice ending to my visit.

Godolphin House, Cornwall

BURNET ROSE (*Rosa pimpinellifolia*)

Henry VIII built Pendennis
in the 1540s as part of his
defences against the Papal forces. It
is very well preserved and provides
an excellent vantage point from
which to view the bustling port of
Falmouth below.

Pendennis Castle, Cornwall

TREE MALLOW (*Lavatera arborea*)

I found two more round houses in
the unspoiled village of Veryan.
They were built in Regency times
by a vicar. Legend has it that he
made them without corners so the
devil had nowhere to hide and thus
could nor tempt his daughters!

Round house, Veryan, Cornwall

HOLLY (*Ilex aquifolium*)
SLENDER MULLEIN (*Verbascum virgatum*)

Steeped in history and immortalised by Gilbert and Sullivan in the *Pirates of Penzance*, Penzance, in Cornwall, is the most westerly of English towns. It nestles on the shores of Mounts Bay, which is dominated by the fairytale castle and priory of St Michael's Mount. Local folklore, legend and rhyme, tell tales of smuggling, shipwrecks, mermaids and Piskies, a Cornish good luck fairy which can be seen everywhere, as charms, and on gates and statues.

Enjoying a mild climate, the National Trust Morab and Trengwaiton Gardens are amongst the most beautiful in the country. Palm, banana and acacia trees, tropical plants and the lovely yellow-flowered New Zealand kowhai, all thrive here far from their native homes.

Penzance, Cornwall

KOWHAI (*Sophora microphylla*)
BEDDING DAHLIA

Engine house of the old Giew Mine,
between Sr Ives and Nancledra, Cornwall

FOXGLOVE (*Digitalis purpurea*)
TREE LUPIN (*Lupinus arborius*)
CREEPING BUTTERCUP (*Ranunculus repens*)

These old engine houses and their stacks, mellowed by time and nature, are a reminder of Cornwall's industrial past. They are often overgrown with an abundance of wild flowers carpeting the magnificent natural rock gardens.

Not far from where the "devil shy" vicar lived is the fishing village of Portloe, which provides yet another happy hunting ground for artists and photographers.

Porrloe, Cornwall

EVERLASTING PEA (*Lathyrus latifolius*)
LAVENDER (*Lavandula officinalis*)

Like Mont St Michael off the coast of Normandy, St Michael's Mount of the Cornish coast is a dramatic sight whether on a sunny or stormy day. Both have similar origins for they were administered by Benedictine monks who used them as Christian trading centres. King Edward the Confessor built a chapel on the latter in the 12th century and, together with additions made in the 17th century, this was incorporated into the castle we see today which was built in the 19th century. It was an important base for the early tin trade.

I can think of no better way to end a day than to see the Mount silhouetted against the famed Cornish sunset.

St Michaels' Mount, Cornwall

GLADIOLUS (Gladiolus colvillei)
WALLFLOWER (Cheiranthus cheiri)
HYDRANGEA (Hydrangea macrophylla hortensia)

The granite cliffs of Land's End rise 200 feet above the Atlantic Ocean on one side and the English Channel on the other. A mile and a half away, Longships Lighthouse perches on an isolated outcrop of rocks. It is a lonely place (when there are no tourists, which is rare) of legend and shipwrecks, of tales of smuggling and tin miners burrowing under the sea. It is a place one has to visit.

Land's End and Longships Lighthouse, Cornwall

WESTERN CLOVER (*Trifolium occidentale*)
HOTTENTOT FIG (*Carpobrotus edulis*)
GLADDEN (*Iris foetidissima*)
YELLOW HORNED POPPY (*Glaucium flavum*)
THRIFT (*Armeria maritima*)
SEA CAMPION (*Silene maritima*)
FUCHSIA (*Fuchsia magellanica*)

St Mawes, Cornwall

HONEYSUCKLE or WOODBINE
(*Lonicera periclymenum*)

St Mawes is a very popular yachting centre in a pretty, sheltered setting, overlooked by another castle built by Henry VIII to defend himself from possible attack by the Papists and the French.

The publishers acknowledge their indebtedness to the following books and journals which were consulted for reference.
AA *Treasures of Britain*
Hand-picked tours in Britain, Automobile Association,
Illustrated Guide to Britain, Automobile Association.
Cook, Olive, *English Cottages and Farmhouses*, Thames & Hudson.
Country Life Picture Book of Britain in Colour, Country Life Ltd.
Court, A.N., *Devon in Colour*, Jarrold & Sons Ltd.
Devon Woodlands, Devon County Council.
Engelmann, F, *The British Scene*, Country Life Ltd.
Hinde, J., *Beautiful Cornwall*.
H.M.S.O., "Historic Places in the Care of the Department of Environment West Country."
Macoboy, S., *What Flower is That?*, Weldon.
Paron, J.A., *Flowers of the Cornish Coast*, Tor Mark Press.
Pope, Rita Tregellas, *The Visitor's Guide to Cornwall*, Hunter Publishing.
Reader's Digest AA Book of the Road, Hodder & Stoughton.
Salisbury District, "Touring in Historic Wessex from Salisbury".
Tomblin, E.W.F., *The Church of Sr Morwenna and Sr John the Baptist*.